2011 Sonora Broncos

Scrimmages

Broncos Are Ready
By Ray Glasscock

To prepare for the 2011 Bronco football season, the Broncos played in two scrimmages. During a scrimmage, the sub-varsity players wear their practice jerseys. This year the varsity players wore jerseys with numbers, but the jersey numbers are not the ones that they will wear once the season starts.

The Broncos played the Llano Yellow Jackets in Llano on August 13. This was a controlled scrimmage where the coaches from both teams were on the field providing instant instruction to the players. At Llano, the Freshman and JV teams ran 20 offensive plays and 20 defensive plays.

It was hard to keep track of scoring since the Freshman and JV were playing at the same time. To the best of my knowledge, the Freshman scored four touchdowns and allowed two. One of the Freshman's touchdowns was scored on a bruising run up the middle by Elijah Cross. Scott Gonzalez scored on a broken field quarterback keeper for the JV.

The Varsity scored four touchdowns, but one may have been called back. Dallas Payne scored twice. He scored on a short run on the spread version of the flanker reverse. Imoni Cross and Payne also combined for an option play that covered about 70 yards. Clayton Parks completed a touchdown pass to Davis Jimenez.

Parks also completed a long pass to Word Hudson to give the Broncos a first and goal. Edward Garza got the score on a run up the middle.

The defense looked very sharp. Freshman Elijah Cross and Junior Blake Esparza had sacks.

The Varsity ran 48 offensive plays: 20 passes and 28 runs. The Broncos had 331 yards of offense with 164 yards rushing and 167 yards passing.

Last Thursday, the Broncos traveled to Grape Creek for their final scrimmage with the Bangs Dragons. The Freshman scored their first touchdown on their third play. Brett Castillo ran off tackle for about 15 yards and was tackled at the one. Andres Acevedo got the touchdown on the quarterback delayed keeper.

On the second drive, Acevedo scrambled for a nice gain. Elijah Cross gained more yardage leaving the touchdown for Acevedo on the quarterback keeper. Castillo scored the last Freshman touchdown.

The only score for the JV Broncos came on a long pass from Scott Gonzales to a wide receiver.

During the controlled portion of the varsity action, Bangs started on offense. On their first play, they gained 24 yards on a running play and a first down. During the remainder of their 60 offensive plays, they made only one other first down. On four of their drives, they lost yardage. The Bronco defense was playing at mid-season form.

When the Broncos were on offense, they were able to move the ball well, but two promising drives ended on interceptions. The Broncos got their only touchdown on a pass from Imoni Cross to Dallas Payne. The play covered about 40 yards with the speedy Payne doing most of the work.

During the live quarter, the Bronco defense held the Dragons to only one first down. Imoni Cross exhibited his broken field running abilities as he three times scrambled for big plays.

Cadesman Pope had a big defensive play as he knocked down a Bangs' pass from his defensive end position. On offense he caught two passes for critical gains. Edward Garza scored the only touchdown during the live quarter on a 15-yard run. Kade Wimberley kicked the PAT.

During the overtime simulation, Cross scrambled for an apparent touchdown, but it was called back for holding.

Facing third and 24, Cross scrambled his way to the open field and threw to Word Hudson for a 14 yard gain. On fourth down, he passed to Pope who caught the ball short of the first down. He refused to go down and drug the defenders for enough yardage for the first down. Once again, Garza got the touchdown on a 13 yard run. This time the PAT was wide right.

When Bangs went on offense, it looked like the Bronco defense was going to have it too easy. On third and long, a sack was judged to be a roughing the passer penalty instead. This gave the Dragons a first and goal from the eight yardline. After three plays, the Dragons had gained three yards. On fourth down, Damon Evans sacked the quarterback ending the overtime.

Broncos Leash The Bulldogs
By Ray Glasscock

The Standard Times picked this game as one of their "Games Of The Week." They chose wisely.

Brady won the toss and elected to receive. The opening drives for each team resulted in three and outs. After a short Bronco punt, the Bulldogs started their first scoring drive on the Bronco 48 yard line. Brady is one of the few teams that still runs the Wing T offense. With the proper players, it is still a potent offense. Linebacker Zach Badeaux said, "We prepared for their running game with extensive tackling practice." It took the Bulldogs ten running plays and one pass play to score their touchdown. Jacob Hodges scored on a two-yard run. Anthony Villarreal kicked the PAT, and the Bulldogs led 7 to 0 with 2:12 left in the first quarter.

Eric Santana fielded the bouncing Bulldog kickoff three yards deep in the end zone. He elected to return the kickoff. He was untouched until he reached the 25 yard line

where several Bulldogs closed around him. Santana refused to go down and he drug several would be tacklers another seven yards to the Bronco 32 yard line. Imoni Cross caught a pass from Clayton Parks on third down for the first Bronco first down. However, the Bulldog defense stopped this drive and forced another punt. Once again, the Bronco punt resembled a pop fly and went only eight yards.

Starting from their 48 yard line, Andrew Brooks gained twenty yards on the power sweep to the right. As the quarter changed, the Bulldogs continued to gain big chunks of yardage with each carry. Brooks ran wide three more times averaging well over six yards per carry. From the Bronco 15 yard line, Travis Sammons took the inside handoff on the wingback counter play to the Bronco one yard line. Santana delayed the touchdown with a strong tackle throwing the larger Sammons out of bounds. A holding penalty against Brady gave the Bronco defense some hope of stopping the drive as the ball was moved back to the twelve yard line. Quarterback Logan Owens tossed a short pass to Brooks who was tackled at the goal line. Owens scored on the sneak and, after the PAT, the Dogs had a 14 to 0 lead with 6:50 in the first half.

Edward Garza returned the kickoff 18 yards to the Bronco 43 yard line. This drive demonstrated the strengths of the Broncos' spread offense. Parks took the snap and pump faked to his right. Then he threw left to Word Hudson. Kyle Patlan and Kade Wimberley provided the blocks allowing Hudson to get past the linebackers and cornerback. Hudson bowled over a defender, and Patlan continued his blocking 20 yards past the line of scrimmage. Even Parks hustled down field to throw a block. Hudson gained 37 yards on the play. On the next play, Parks threw right to Zach Badeaux who had no trouble avoiding Dog defenders for the 20 yard touchdown reception and the first Bronco touchdown of the 2011 season. Wimberley kicked the PAT and suddenly a two play drive changed a two touchdown lead to one with 6:13 left in the first half.

Santana returned the second half kickoff to the Bulldog 45-yard line. Cross ran twice, Hudson landed on his head after a catch, Cadesman Pope juggled and then caught a Parks' pass, Cross ran to the two, and Badeaux ran untouched through a huge hole for the Bronco touchdown. The blocking scheme featured Pope blocking to the inside from his end position and Wimberley blocking to the outside from his

tackle position. Coach Sine called a play designed to cause massive confusion for the defense which resulted in an easy pass from Cross to Pope for the two point conversion. With 7:41 left in the third quarter, the Broncos led 15 to 14. Since I was videoing from the Brady stands, the Brady fans could sense the outcome of this game.

"During half time, Kyle (Patlin) and a few other seniors provided the inspiration that we (the defense) needed," said defensive lineman Blake Esparza. In the second half, the Brady Wing T plays were no longer fooling the Broncos. Badeaux said, "We

started anticipating their plays and filled up the holes." Also, Brooks suffered an apparent knee injury and had to leave the game.

The Broncos took over in Bulldog territory when Brady tried a fake punt that failed to make a first down. After a Cross carry, Parks threw his second touchdown pass to Badeaux that covered 36 yards. Kimberley kicked the PAT making the score 22 to 14 with 2:33 left in the third quarter.

The next Bulldog drive lasted only three plays as Esparza recovered a fumble giving the Broncos another short field at the Bulldog 22 yard line. Parks pump faked and then threw his third varsity touchdown to Hudson. The Broncos lead 28 to 14 with 1:24 left in the third quarter as the PAT kick was wide

Esparza recovered his second fumble. The Bulldogs were able to stop this Bronco drive. Wimberley kicked a 31-yard field goal to make the final score 31 to 14 in favor of the Broncos with 9:13 left in the game. Wimberley's kick would have easily been good from the 45-yard line!

This matchup was a game of two distinctly different halves. Senior Dallas Payne said, "We went into the locker room at halftime embarrassed with our play, but we wanted this victory more which made the difference."

The Broncos travel to Forsan on Friday to take on the 1-0 Buffaloes on their new Carter 419 artificial turf system. Game time is 7:30.

Forsan JV – September 1, 2011

JV Buffaloes Fall to JV Broncos
By Nancy Glasscock

After a back and forth game last week against the Brady Bulldogs JV team, the JV Broncos had to duplicate it again against the Forsan Buffaloes. The first quarter of the game ended in a scoreless stalemate. Both defense stopped all offensive drives.

Forsan got on the scoreboard first with a 55 yard run up the middle for a touchdown by Kolby Self. Quarterback To'a MauMau tossed a quick pitch to Self for the two point conversion. The Buffaloes led 8 to 0 with 8:26 left in the second quarter.

The Broncos answered with a 67 yard drive of their own. Scott Gonzales, Will Dutton, and Austin Rodriguez systematically worked the ball down the field with runs of ten yards or more. Once the Broncos reached a first goal at the three yard line, the Broncos shifted to the I formation and Rodriguez got the touchdown by going through the hole opened by the right tackle. Gonzales rolled to his left and

threw the two point conversion pass to Rhett Guerra. With 4:58 left in the first half, the score was tied at 8. There was no more scoring in the first half.

In the third quarter, the Buffaloes got the lead back with MauMau throwing a long pass to Ryan Pearson. On the next play, MauMau got the touchdown on the quarterback keeper from 25 yards out. This was the last play of the third quarter and the score stood at 14 to 8 in favor of the Buffaloes.

Guerra took the kickoff and gained 30 yards to the Buffalo 40 yard line. Gonzales dropped back to pass. He was forced to scramble and he gained 20 yards. Hagen Kennedy made a one-handed catch for the next big gain. Rodriguez ran to the 12 yard line setting up a touchdown pass to Dutton in the left corner of the end zone. Dutton also scored the two point conversion on an off tackle run to the right making the score 16 to 14 in favor of the Broncos.

Forsan's next drive to regain the lead stalled. With about two minutes left in the game, the Broncos needed to run out the clock to win the game. The Broncos ran three plays that gained nothing and the Buffaloes used their timeouts wisely. On fourth down on their own 35 yard line, Gonzales ran to his left. Kennedy provided the block that sprung Gonzales for a 65 yard game clinching touchdown.

The two point play was no good – but that didn't matter. The Broncos won 22 to 14 to earn their second victory and remain undefeated. The JV team travels to Ballinger to play the JV Bearcats on Thursday.

Forsan – September 2, 2011

Broncos Stampede The Buffaloes
By Ray Glasscock

With the windmills turning to the backdrop of the setting sun, the Sonora Broncos took the field at Forsan for the inaugural varsity game on the Buff's new artificial turf field. After the first two series, there was no doubt who was going to win the ball game. The play of the Broncos, both offensively and defensively, was a thing of beauty. However, the Forsan stadium and radio announcers also provided some comical moments and many interesting and complimentary comments on the Broncos' play. According to the stadium announcers, Braxton Synder and Chance Campbell handled the quarterbacking duties for the Broncos. Granted, our jersey numbers are difficult to read. Once the game was out of hand, Clayton Parks and Imoni Cross got some time playing quarterback.

The Broncos won the toss after the officials read the entire rulebook to the respective captains. The officials could have easily flagged themselves for delay of game.

On the third play of the game, Cross dropped back, rolled right away from the defenders and tossed a short receiver screen pass to Zach Badeaux. Badeaux hurdled a tackler and sped untouched to complete the 50 yard pass and catch for the game's first touchdown.

Kade Wimberley (aka Braxton Snyder) kicked the PAT and the scoreboard read 7 to 0 in the Broncos' favor with 11:05 left in the first quarter.

With three of the four members of Forsan's state qualifying 4x100 relay team on the field, Coach Sine and his staff knew that they had good speed. The game plan to stop their speed was quite successful. Cross kicked off high and short forcing them to fair catch the kickoffs. The defense blitzed and blitzed. Damon Evans got the game started with a tackle for a loss on Foster Burchett, the Forsan quarterback. The Bronco line played great all night either making the tackle or allowing the linebackers to attack the runners untouched. The first Forsan series was an R cubed P. (Run, run, run, punt).

After an excellent punt, the Broncos started on their own 17 yard line. Parks threw to Cadesman Pope for a first down and then twice to Word Hudson.

The second pass to Hudson covered 46 yards to the Buff's ten yard line. Badeaux got the touchdown on a run up the middle. My video showed that Bryce Smith pancaked the nose guard, Blaise Coffman (5'7" – 238 pounds), Lino Villanueva took Tyler Roach, the inside linebacker into the endzone, Ricky Samaniego knocked Polo Morin, the outside linebacker to the turf and Michael Sanchez and Kyle Patlin doubled teamed linebacker Patrick Robles which provided the hole for Badeaux. Ty Johnson, the fastest player on the field, blocked the PAT, and the score stood at 13 to 0 with 8:32 left in the first quarter.

Cross kicked off deep. Pope and Eric Santana tacked Johnson at the Forsan 22 yard line. At this point, the KXCS announcer commented, "If the Buffs are able to stretch this out (drive), it would be a huge moral victory." On third down, Burchett scrambled for a Buffaloes first down. Campbell stopped the next run, Sam Powers knocked down a pass on second down, and Jesse Vasquez forced a desperation pass to Roman who was tackled from behind short of the first down by Pope.

Cross got the next Bronco drive going with a scramble of 20 yards. Edward Garza raced for a 29 yard gain to the their 28 yard line. Parks executed the flanker screen to Pope who rambled toward the end zone, but Burchett was able to force him out of bounds at the half yard line. Garza got the touchdown on the next play. Coach Sine called the exact same play for the two point conversion and Garza delivered.

The score was 21 to 0 with 3:59 left in the first quarter. The radio announcers commented: "Forsan didn't know what to look for or who to cover. We don't know where the next punch is coming from."

During the next defensive series, Powers blocked his second pass of the game. After one first down, Forsan punted to the Broncos.

On third down, Parks passed to Garza who moved the sticks from the 16 to 30. Parks followed up with a 30 yard completion to Cross who made a leaping catch between Johnson and Roman. Parks to Pope gained 20 yards. This Bronco drive stalled when Johnson got a hand on a Parks' pass to Hudson at the goal line, and Parks was sacked on fourth down.

The next three and out featured Synder blocking a Burchett pass. Cross fair caught the Buffalo punt at the Broncos 40 yard line. Garza rushed for a first down and Forsan. Cross ran the quarterback dive and was tackled at the one yard line. Cross got the touchdown on the next carry up the middle.

Wimberley kicked the PAT making the score 28 to 0 with 7:29 left in the second quarter.

The Forsan's offensive coordinator's nightmare continued. With the Bronco line completely dominating, he tried a screen pass on third down. Watching the video, it was clear that the Bronco defense had some tell on when they were going to run the screen. Hudson was ready and delivered his customary, hard hit of the game.

Cross was able to field the Buff's next punt and returned it about ten yards to the Forsan 38 yard line. Parks rolled to his left and threw to Cross who raced untouched for the fifth Bronco touchdown. Wimberley kicked it true and the score was 35 to 0 with 5:33 left in the first half. The radio announcers had this to say: "Parks looks like Peyton Manning in the shotgun changing the play."

Right before halftime, the Broncos scored again. Parks hit Garza for a 20 yard gain and then followed up with a 40 yard touchdown pass to Cross.

Wimberley finished the first half scoring with a successful PAT making the score 42 to 0 at the half. The radio announcers commented, "As I watch them (Broncos) play and think back to the preseason pick of San Saba (picked number one), if they are better than the Broncos, that's going to be an unbelievable matchup."

In the second half, Forsan got a touchdown against the first string defense on a blown coverage pass play. Burchett completed a long touchdown pass to his brother Trevor Burchett. Their PAT was good and the score was 42 to 7 with 8:55 left in the third.

Parks threw his third touchdown pass to Hudson.

Wimberley finished the Bronco scoring making the score 49 to 7 with 3:17 left in the third quarter. Again, another compliment from the radio announcers: "You see right there, their execution through the air is just unbelievable."

In the fourth quarter, Forsan scored two touchdowns and one safety which made the final score 49 to 23.

Parks completed 15 of 21 passes for 284 yards and three touchdowns. Cross threw a 50 yard touchdown pass, caught two touchdown passes, and ran for a touchdown and a two point conversion. Garza led all rushers with 105 yards on eight carries. The Broncos had 182 yards rushing and 334 yards passing for a total of 516 total yards of offense. The passing yardage came on 16 completions for a 20.88 average.

Nine Broncos had tackles for a loss, Powers and Evans had sacks, and ten Broncos had hurries. Evans led all tacklers with 16 and Jorge Villanueva was second with 14.

This week the Broncos are at home and play the 0 – 2 Ballinger Bearcats.

Bronco Freshmen Win Rematch
By Nancy Glasscock

The rematch between the Wall Hawks freshman and the Bronco freshman teams started with a bang.

Multi-purpose player, Elijah Cross took the first handoff 84 yards up the Hawks' side of the field for the initial touchdown. Cross also kicked the PAT. Only 29 seconds came off the clock and the Broncos led 7 to 0.

The Hawks appeared to be on their way to tying the score as their opening drive reached the red zone before the Broncos stopped them. After that drive, both teams had short drives and traded punts.

Brett Castillo intercepted a long bomb at the goal line to stop the next red zone drive by the Hawks. Andres Acevedo then sent Castillo on a crossing pattern for a big reception. Even though the drive stalled, the big pass play changed the field position in the Broncos' favor. When the drive stalled, Acevedo punted and just missed a coffin corner punt as the ball just missed going out of bounds at the one yard line.

When the Broncos stopped the Hawks, the Broncos started their next scoring drive. Passes to Castillo, Bryan Garcia, Sid Anderson, and Cross highlighted the drive. Cross, stiff arming and dragging defenders, advanced the ball into the Hawks' red zone for a first and goal. The Hawks stiffened. On fourth and goal from the 13 yard line, Acevedo threw a touchdown pass to Castillo who made a diving catch that just got the ball over the end line for a touchdown. The coaches called for a fake PAT kick and Acevedo ran it in for the two point conversion making the score 15 to 0.

Once again, the Hawks tried to get back in the game, but the Bronco defense and the play clock ended the next Hawk drive and the score was 15 to 0 at the end of the half.

The Broncos kicked off to start the second half. Smelling blood, the Bronco defense led by Castillo, Sid Anderson, Cross, Acevedo, Brian Garcia, Michael Gonzales and Ethan Patlan stopped the Hawks forcing them to punt. When the Hawk punter couldn't handle the deep snap, he was tackled for a big loss.

Acevedo took matters into his on hand and ran for a 25 yard touchdown. When the PAT failed, the score stood at 21 to 0 with 3 seconds left in the 3rd quarter.

Again, Castillo, Acevedo, Seth Gunn, Tanner Esparza, created chaos for the Hawk offense. Half way through the fourth quarter, Patlin recovered a Hawk fumble. Anderson, Castillo and Cross advanced the ball down the field to set up the fourth Sonora touchdown. Cross smashed his way to a one yard touchdown run. The PAT kick was good and the Broncos led 28 to 0 with 4:51 left in the game.

After a "pass interference" call against Sonora, Wall scored their only touchdown on a well thrown pass and catch. The Hawk holder could not handle the PAT snap and Patlin tackled the kicker as he tried to salvage the situation.

Wall then tried an onsides kick, but Sonora covered it. With a short field, Cross bulled his way to the Hawk 19 yard line. Castillo took the handoff and ran wide to his right for the last Bronco touchdown. The snap for the PAT was high, so Acevedo just tossed it to Cross who ran for the two point conversion. At 3:29 left in the game, the Broncos led 36 to 6.

The Hawk kickoff returner fumbled, and the Broncos ran out the clock to end the game. The freshman Broncos, now 2-1, play Fredricksburg next Thursday in Fredericksburg.

Ballinger – September 9, 2011

Broncos Crush Bearcats
By Ray Glasscock

It is highly likely that the Sonora Broncos set an all time record this week against the Ballinger Bearcats by scoring 54 points in the first half. Everything that the Sonora coaches called worked, and nothing the Ballinger coaches called succeeded.

The Broncos had nine opportunities to score and they scored eight touchdowns! Clayton Parks completed 19 of 29 passes for 266 yards and three touchdowns. Word Hudson caught six passes for 95 yards while Zach Badeaux snagged six passes for 67 yards. Edward Garza was the leading rusher with 57 yards on 13 carries followed by Erik Santana with 50 yards on eight carries. There were 19 Broncos who made tackles with Damon Evans leading the way with two solo tackles and ten assists. Badeaux, Sam Powers, Evans and Dallas Payne had sacks.

On defense, the Broncos held the Bearcats to 48 yards of passing offense. The Ballinger quarterback completed four passes out of 16 attempts with one pick six interception. Their leading rusher carried the ball 12 times and gained 21 yards. With the Broncos making four sacks, the Bearcats finished the game with 18 carries for a negative four yards!

The only time that the Broncos failed to score in the first half was on the opening drive. On the second drive, Parks hit Payne with a 50 yard completion, followed by a 21 yard completion to Badeaux. Badeaux scored on a one yard touchdown run through a HUGE hole opened by 800 pounds of Bronco blocking provided by Evans, Kade Wimberley, Kyle Patlin, and Cadesman Pope. The Broncos tried to run for the two point conversion, but it was stopped.

The second scoring drive started at the Bearcats 38 yard line setup by a 12 yard punt return by Imoni Cross.

After three incomplete passes, the Broncos lined up in punt formation. Parks threw to Payne for a 22 yard gain to the Bearcats 16 yard line. Badeaux covered the remaining yardage on an eleven yard catch and a five yard touchdown run.

Garza added two points on a run up the middle.

Hudson scored the next touchdown on a leaping catch in the end zone. Wimberley kicked the PAT making the score 21 to 0 with two seconds left in the first quarter.

In the next drive, Garza made up for a sack with a big gain on a draw play, Cross caught a pass for a first down, Pope's reception moved the ball into the red zone, and Hudson duplicated his first touchdown catch with another leaping reception in the end zone. Wimberley kicked and the score keeper updated the scoreboard to show Broncos 28 and Visitor 0 with 9:25 left in the second quarter.

Payne stopped Hudson's two game streak for the hardest hit of the game. Payne hit a Bearcat defender just as the ball arrived causing the incompletion forcing the Bearcats to punt.

Parks opened the next drive with two long passes to the leaping Hudson.

Parks tossed his third touchdown pass to Pope. The Ballinger crowd cheered when a Bearcat blocked the PAT kick and the Broncos led by 34 points with 6:51 left in the first half.

Blake Esparza recovered a Bearcat fumble. Three plays later, Garza got his second touchdown on a one yard run. The PAT kick was wide making the score 40 to 0 with 4:40 left in the second quarter.

Ballinger's sophomore quarterback overthrew his receiver and Cross started his interception return at the Bronco 29 yard line. The elusive Cross took it 71 yards for a touchdown.

After Wimberley's kick, the scoreboard read 47 to 0 with 3:29 left in the first half.

Jorge Villanueva recovered a fumble. Santana ran the sweep for the last touchdown of the game.

Wimberley scored the 54th point of the half with a perfect kick. I can't tell for sure, but I think the Bearcat band played the old Hee Haw song "if it weren't for bad luck, I would have no luck at all."

The Broncos are now 3 and 0 for the season. This week is homecoming and the Broncos will be hosting the Bracket Tigers.

Brackettville – September 15,2011

Broncos Shutout Tigers
By Ray Glasscock

Never before have the Sonora Broncos recorded consecutive shutoffs AND scored more than 50 points per game! It was no surprise to anyone that the Broncos were going to beat the outmatched Brackettville Tigers. As usual, the Tigers were well coached, played sound football, and were tough as nails. I don't think that I have ever seen a Tiger leave the field with an injury that was short of a compound fracture or a severed artery.

The explosive Bronco offense is compiling some very confusing statistics. The Broncos managed only 12 first downs while scoring 56 points. Clayton Parks threw for 255 yards on 14 of 23 passes which is an 18.21 yards per catch average.

The Broncos rushed 25 times for 128 yards. It is not uncommon to read box scores where a losing team will have many more first downs and more rushing yardage. Edward Garza led all rushers with 56 yards on eight carries. Seven Broncos carried the pigskin during the game. Erik Santana, Zach Badeaux, and Garza averaged over seven yards per carry. Parks completed passes to nine different receivers. Cadesman Pope was the leading receiver with three catches for 95 yards and one 62 yard touchdown.

Word Hudson caught two passes for 61 yards and both of them were for touchdowns. Dallas Payne caught one pass for 12 yards and a touchdown.

On defense, the Broncos' speed, size, and strength completely dominated the Tiger offense. The Tigers gained 42 yards passing by completing 3 of 8 passes. They ran the ball 32 times for a MINUS 23 yards. They managed two first downs and 19 yards of total offense. Their leading rusher gained seven yards on two carries. Nineteen Broncos recorded tackles. Damon Evans led with 12 tackles followed by Badeaux with 11. Five of Evans' tackles were for losses, and Kyle Patlan had four for losses. Kade Wimberley had the only sack, and Badeaux had an interception.

The first Bronco scoring drive used nine plays highlighted by pass receptions by Pope, Cross, and Davis Jimenez. Hudson got the touchdown on a five yard reception. Wimberley missed his PAT kick and the score was 6 to 0 with 8:47 left in the first quarter.

It took only two plays for the next Bronco score. Pope scored on a 62 yard catch and run.

Wimberley made up for his miss when he smashed through the Tigers for the two point conversion. 14 to 0 with 4:10 left in the first quarter.

The next Bronco score was setup when Badeaux blocked a Tiger punt giving the ball to the Broncos on the Tiger's eleven yard line. Payne caught his first touchdown pass of the season on third down. Parks threw the ball where Payne had to leap to catch it in the back corner of the end zone. Wimberley's kick made the score 21 to 0 with 8:46 left in the second quarter.

Imoni Cross returned a punt for an apparent touchdown, but it was called back on a penalty. Four plays later, Hudson scored his second touchdown on a 54 yard reception for Parks.

The kick was good and the score moved to 28 to 0 with 5:10 left in the half.

In the second half, Braxton Snyder caught a 15 yard pass on fourth down to keep a drive alive. Garza scored on a 25 yard run. With 6:35 left in the third, the score was 35 to 0.

Jimenez scored on a fumble recovery. When the Tiger center centered the ball over his quarterback's head, Santana hit the quarterback as he was trying to pick up the ball allowing Jimenez to scoop it up and score.

After a five yard penalty, Wimberley had to kick from further back, and he still boomed it through. 42 to 0 with 5:28 left in the third.

The next drive and score belonged to Badeaux. He intercepted, took an excellent option pitch from Cross to the Tigers' eleven yard line, ran the sweep to the two, and scored on a dive. 49 to 0 with 2:50 left in the third.

The last score of the game was setup by an outstanding broken field run by Santana. Wimberley got the score on an eleven yard run. After the touchdown, Cross kicked the PAT making the final score 56 to 0.

This week the Broncos travel to Blanco for the rubber match with the Panthers as the modern era series is tied at two apiece. Take a road trip and support the Broncos in their last non-district game.

Blanco – September 23, 2011

Bronco Defense Dominates Panthers
By Ray Glasscock

The game between the Sonora Broncos and the Blanco Panthers couldn't have been more exciting for the players, fans, and coaches. We all knew that it would be a great game between two very good and well-prepared football teams. I am sure that the Sonora coaches were determined to stop the big running plays including the wrap around draw and the flanker trap. Coach Rogers had a defensive plan that was designed to stop our passing attack. It appears to me that Blanco is good at stopping the run since it's second nature to them. I had expected them to put maximum pressure on Clayton Parks, but they chose instead to rush four linemen and drop seven into coverage. Last year's game will be remembered for many, many years for the impossible last drive as Ethan Morriss scored with no time left. While this game was exciting, it would not be long remembered if the morph play had not happened. Years from now, people will ask, "Were you at the morph game against Blanco?"

The Bronco defense has dominated every previous game, and the coaches were hoping to find out how the Broncos would hold up against the Blanco Panthers. So how did the defense do? There were 78 tackles in the game with ten being solo tackles. That means that 68 tackles were the "host of Broncos" type of tackles.

Dallas Payne led all tacklers with ten tackles all of the assist variety. Ryan San Miguel, Imoni Cross, and Word Hudson made two solo tackles each while Jorge Villanueva, Zach Badeaux, Kyle Patlan, and Cadesman Pope had one solo tackle each.

The Broncos held the Panthers to ten first downs, 60 yards of rushing, and 140 yards of passing. The Panthers scored one touchdown. Tyler Brown was their leading rusher with 32 yards on six carries.

Offensively, the Broncos logged more first downs and more yardage than in any previous game, but scored fewer points. The Broncos had only six first downs in the first half, but exploded for 17 in the second half. While Blanco held the Broncos to 95 yards rushing,

Parks and his receiving corps amassed 342 yards. Parks completed 27 of 38 passes while throwing his first interception of the year. Parks spread his passes among five receivers: Cross caught four for 66 yards, Badeaux had five for 32, Garza had two for seven, Hudson had 7 for seventy, and Pope led all receivers with 9 receptions for 167 yards and one touchdown. Cross was the leading rusher with 69 yards on 12 carries. He would have had more yardage except that for the third game in a row, he had a touchdown called back due to Bronco penalties.

On Blanco's opening drive, they were stopped when Cross intercepted Tanner Rogers and returned it 39 yards. The first Bronco offensive series had Hudson catching a fourth down pass to move the chains, Garza getting it to the five yard line on a shovel pass, and it ended when Parks threw his first interception of the season.

Taking over at their own five yard line, the Panthers were able to move it to their 45 before having to punt. Rogers boomed a punt that went out of bounds at the Broncos five yard line.

After being stopped, Parks had to punt. Sam Isenberg returned it to the Bronco 35 yard line. Rogers had his longest run of the night when he gained 9 yards on the keeper. Brown ripped off Blanco's longest run of the night when he gained 13 yards setting up a first and goal. The drive ended when Rogers was stripped of the pigskin as he was struggling for yardage. Payne came up with drive ending recovery at the Bronco eleven yard line.

Badeaux got the Broncos a first down on a quick pass from Parks as he almost broke it down the sideline. Hudson had one tackle busting run after catch as he gained 15 yards. Badeaux then started in motion and took out a line backer allowing Garza to get good yardage and a first down. Pope caught his first two passes of the night.

Cross caught a throw back screen and used his broken field instincts to give the Broncos a first down at the Panthers' 18 yard line.

The drive stalled and Kade Wimberley kicked a 34 yard field goal to give the Broncos a 3 to 0 lead with 3:47 left in the first half.

After another defensive stop by the Broncos, Rogers once again backed us up with another great punt that went out of bounds on the Broncos 13 yard line. As I have reviewed my videos of the games, I have noticed that not all snaps to Parks have been perfect. It just seems that he has an uncanny ability to field the snap and go right on with the play. Then, I was reminded that Parks is an All West Texas catcher. But even so, sometimes there are wild pitches/passed balls. The snap was low and went between Parks' legs. He retrieved the ball and tried to throw the ball out of bounds. Since the ball didn't get beyond the line of scrimmage and he was throwing from within his endzone, it was charged as a safety. The score at the end of the half was 3 to 2 in favor of Sonora.

Erik Santana got the second half off to a good start when he returned the Panthers' kickoff to the 32 yard line. Coach Sine changed his approach. This drive featured Parks throwing shorter passes to Hudson and Pope, and Cross running from the Wildcat formation. After three Cross' runs resulted in two first downs, Parks once again threw deep over the middle. A Blanco defender tipped the ball and Pope caught it on the rebound for a 30+ yard gain giving the Broncos a first down at the Panthers' eleven yard line. On third down, Cross leaped for a touchdown, but the ball came out. It was ruled that the ground caused the ball to come out and the

Broncos had a first and goal inside the one. The Broncos lined up in the heavy formation with Evans and Wimberley set to block for Badeaux. However, Parks ran the quarterback sneak and scored. The Broncos led 9 to 2 with 6:17 left in the third quarter after the PAT kick was wide right.

Blanco managed one first down before they had to punt. Cross took the snap and immediately had to avoid a Panther. He got away and started to his right. When he was trapped by the sideline and several Panthers, he used his patented spin move to break free and start up the Blanco sideline with a shoulder pad flapping. The Panthers swarmed around Cross.

Somehow, Cross managed to MORPH into Hudson's body to continue his run. Cross went into the pile, but Hudson came out with the ball and gained another 15 yards.

Nine plays later, the Broncos attempted a 26 yard field goal, but it was not good.

The Panthers started a drive that was looking good for them. Then they were flagged for a chop block and the fifteen yard penalty forced them out to throw the ball. Hudson separated a Blanco receiver from the ball with a HARD hit and the Panthers had to punt.

After another excellent punt, the Broncos started a 96 yard scoring drive. The drive took seven plays. There were six completed passes and one running play. Cross caught a quick pass and turned it into a 25 yard gain. Pope got the touchdown on a leaping catch over a much shorter defender. After Wimberley made his PAT kick, the score was 16 to 2 in favor of the Broncos with 4:35 left.

Turn about is fair play. Needing to throw, the Panthers completed two long passes. Hudson was able to tip one of the passes, but it fell into the receiver's hands for a long gain. Then, Cross leaped but couldn't keep the receiver from catching a touchdown for the Panthers. After the PAT, the score was 16 to 9 with 3:19 left in the game.

The final drive of the game featured three amazing plays. Parks was forced out of the pocket and started to run. Then he saw Pope just a few feet in front of him. He tossed a short pass to Pope who split the defenders for a 30 yard gain to the Panthers' 43 yard line. Cross fielded a low snap, avoided the first line of defenders, and weaved his way for an apparent touchdown. For the third week in a row, Cross had a touchdown called back for a Bronco penalty.

The chess match between the coaches continued. Coach Sine called for the Broncos to take a knee. No time out from Coach Rogers. Coach Sine called for another knee. Then Rogers called a time out. The Broncos now faced 3rd and 20 with the prospect of the Panthers getting the ball back. Parks calmly took the snap and threw deep for Pope who caught the ball for a first down.

The next kneel down ended the game with the final score of 16 to 9. The Broncos are now 5 and 0 going into district.

The Broncos are off this week. On October 7th, the Broncos travel to Junction to start District 13-2A play. Sonora leads this series 49-20-3. Game time is 7:30 PM.

Junction – October 7, 2011

Broncos Soar Over Eagles
By Ray Glasscock

There is an old saying about eavesdroppers: you might not like what you hear. I am not sure if listening to the Junction radio announcers broadcasting the game is really eavesdropping, but they made the comment that the Junction Eagles don't really like the Broncos from Sonora. I think I can understand as the all time win loss record reads 50 wins, 20 losses, and 3 ties in favor of Sonora. Sonora's 50th win over Junction was by a score of 59 to 0. To make matters worse for Junction, Kade Wimberley led all Bronco scorers with 17 points on eight PAT kicks, one field goal, and one touchdown. I am sure Kade and his parents must have mixed feelings about his night.

The stats for this contest tell the story of a completely outmatched opponent. The Broncos scored 35 points in the first quarter, 17 points in the second, and 7 points in the third quarter. Sonora scored on every opportunity until Junction stopped a scoring drive at the beginning of the fourth quarter. The Broncos had 23 first downs, no turnovers, 209 yards rushing and 261 yards passing for a total of 470 yards.

Clayton Parks completed 10 of 14 passes for 226 yards with three passes going for touchdowns. His NFL quarterback rating was 153.3. (The maximum NFL quarterback rating is 158.1) Davis Jiminez completed three passes out of nine for 35 yards.

Nine Broncos got to run with ball. Zach Badeaux had eight carries for 52 yards and one touchdown. Edward Garza ran seven times for 58 yards and one touchdown. Jesus Vasquez rushed for 51 yards on six carries.

Parks and Jiminez spread their completions between seven receivers. Badeaux caught four for 50 yards, Garza had one catch for a 26 yard touchdown, Word Hudson caught two for 45 yards with one going for a touchdown, Cadesman Pope caught two for 55 yards with one going for a touchdown, Jiminez had one catch for 50 yards, and Ryan San Miguel snagged one for 14 yards and Rhett Guerra caught two for 21 yards.

Imoni Cross scored the first Bronco touchdown on a 65 yard punt return and Wimberley kicked his first of eight PATs.

Parks was forced out of the pocket and ran to his left. Just prior to reaching the sideline, he signaled for Hudson to go deep. Hudson caught the 26 yard pass from Parks for the touchdown. This scoring drive covered 63 yards on 7 plays and took 2:05 off the clock.

The next Bronco drive lasted three plays, covered 25 yards, lasted 27 seconds, and Garza scored on a seven yard run.

Garza scored on a 28 yard pass from Parks on a three play drive that covered 41 yards and 30 seconds.

The last score of the first quarter featured Wimberley scoring on a five yard run. This drive lasted 40 seconds and covered 55 yards in two plays.

Damon Evans scored his first varsity touchdown on the first drive of the second quarter. He bulled his way into the end zone from one yard out. This drive lasted five plays covering 43 yards and 1:47 worth of game clock time.

Pope, the Broncos' man among boys, scored on shortest (time wise) drive of the game as he caught a 51 yard pass from Parks. This one play drive lasted only eleven seconds.

The last scoring drive of the first half ended when Wimberley kicked a 35 yard field goal. That drive covered 50 yards in six plays and lasted 1:32. The score at the end of the first half was 52 to 0.

Sonora received the second half kickoff. The last scoring drive of the night covered 66 yards on 11 plays and lasted 4:46. Badeaux handled the ball on ten of the 11 plays and he scored the touchdown on a two yard run.

Defensively, the Broncos were equally impressive. 21 Broncos made tackles. Jorge Villanueva, the KHOS defensive player of the game, and San Miguel led the Broncos with eight tackles. Badeaux, Erik Santana, and San Miguel tied for the solo tackle lead with three solo tackles each. Hagen Kennedy, Guerra, Nathan Jarratt, and Alonzo Hernandez, JV players getting their first varsity action, contributed 11 tackles in the fourth quarter that were instrumental in preserving the shutout.

Santana and Blake Esparza had quarterback sacks. Santana and Cross had an interception each. Jiminez recovered two fumbles and Villanueva fell on one.

This week, the road warriors travel to San Saba for what may be the game that decides the district championship. San Saba is 4 and 2 and just shutout Harper by a score of 44 to 0. Both Sonora and San Saba return most of the players who played in last year's game, and Sonora won that game by a score of 34 to 24. The visitor stands at San Saba are quite small, so make the trip and fill them up.

Broncos "Surprise" Armadillos 51 to 23
By Ray Glasscock

"In a district full of dynamic, versatile athletes, it'll be the overlooked Armadillos that prove steady play wins," predicted the forecasters at Dave Campbell's TexasFootball.com. Dave Campbell picked San Saba to win our district based on the fact that San Saba returned their entire offensive and defensive lines. Throughout the first seven weeks of this season, the "experts" on most of the football Internet forums have dismissed the accomplishments of the Broncos. As I was videoing the game and listening to the San Saba radio station, the announcers kept saying how surprised they were at the speed and quickness of the Broncos. Many times they commented that they knew the Broncos could score, but they were almost continuous in their praise of the speed, quickness, and toughness of the Broncos' defense.

The Broncos received the opening kickoff. The Armadillos disrupted the first series by effective blitzing and forced the Broncos into their first three and out since the Forsan game.

After a Clayton Parks' punt, the Dillos started on the 50 yard line. On their second play, Ryan Pannell handed off to Zack Davis on the counter play and he gained 30 yards to the Broncos' 20 yard line. Three plays later, Word Hudson intercepted Pannell in the end zone and returned it to 25 yard line.

After a five yard run by Zach Badeaux, Imoni Cross ran wide from the "wildcat" formation and sped down the right side line for a 70 yard touchdown.

Kade Wimberley (Mr. W) kicked the PAT and the Broncos led 7 to 0 with 7:35 left in the first quarter.

"I have heard about this Imoni Cross. He runs like a quarter horse, can cut on a dime, and give you a nickels change!" commented the San Saba radio announcers.

Later in the game, after a hard hit on a Dillo receiver by Dallas Payne, they commented, "That hit was a slobberknocker!"

The Armadillos started their next drive at their 15 yard line after Jesus Vasquez and friends stopped the kickoff return. The first two runs lost yards. This led to more compliments from the announcers. "We can't really tell who made the tackle for the Broncos, as there are so many white shirts on each tackle. On most plays, there are three Broncos standing and the other eight are getting off our runner." After completing a pass short of the first down, the 'Dillos had to punt and they intentionally kicked it out of bounds keeping it out of Cross's hands.

The Broncos started their drive at their 42 yard line. After one first down, the Dillos' defense stepped up and stuffed some Bronco running plays. Then Parks rolled to his left and threw to Cadesman Pope. The smaller San Saba player committed pass interference, and the penalty kept the drive alive at the San Saba 35 yard line. Parks made the play of the drive when he rolled to his left and was about to be sacked for a loss when he spun away from the tacklers and started back to his right. He spotted Hudson open and threw to him. Hudson almost scored as he was pushed out of bounds inside the five yard line. On the first play of the second quarter, Badeaux scored from one yard out, as all he had to do was follow Kyle Patlan and Damon Evans into the end zone. Mr. W kicked the PAT and the score was 14 to 0 with 11:55 left in the second quarter.

Once again, the Bronco special teams stopped the San Saba returner short of the 20 yard line. Two running plays lost yardage under several Bronco tacklers. Pannell dropped to pass, and Pope hit him as he was trying to pass. The ball popped into the air, and Payne grabbed it for the easiest pick six of his career. After Wimberley's PAT, the Broncos led 21 to 0 with 11:22 left in the second quarter.

Hagen Kennedy led the Bronco tacklers as the San Saba return man was stopped at the 21 yard line. Pannell attempted two passes. One was dropped as Hudson closed for the kill, and Cross leveled the other receiver causing him to drop the ball. On fourth down, the ball was centered over the San Saba punter's head. The punter attempted to kick the ball out of the back of the end zone, but he whiffed. The Broncos just missed recovering for a touchdown, as the ball went out the back of the end zone. Blake Esparza was credited with the safety, and the Dillos were now down 23 to 0 with 9:27 left in the second quarter.

One minute and 27 seconds later, Cross scored on a 33 yard run, and Mr. W kicked the PAT for a 30 to 0 lead with 8:00 minutes left in the first half.

San Saba responded with a nice drive of their own marching to a first and goal. But the Bronco defense stepped up and forced a turnover on downs. San Saba got the ball back as Parks threw his second interception of the season. On third and long, 6' 3" Luke Cox grabbed a pass over 5'4" Ryan San Miguel giving the Dillos a first and goal. They scored on a dive up the middle and, after the PAT, the score stood 30 to 7 with 2:15 left in the first half.

It didn't take the Broncos long to respond. Badeaux had a 30 yard kickoff return. Edward Garza got around the left end for a 15 yard gain. Parks threw deep to Hudson who did his patented leap over the defender to catch the pass. Then he threw the defender to ground and walked into the end zone completing a 42 pass play for a touchdown.

Mr. W kicked the PAT, and the score at the half was 37 to 7 in favor of the Broncos.

In the second half, San Saba scored on a trick play. Pannell handed off to a runner who was going to his right. The runner stopped and threw back to Pannell who scored. After the PAT, the score stood at 37 to 14 with 11:11 left in the third quarter.

San Saba attempted an onsides kick after their score. The ball was kicked at their 40 yard line, and it had such a spin on it that it went out of bounds at their 40 yard line. After a five yard penalty for illegal procedure, the Broncos had a short field. Badeaux gained 17 yards on a run. Parks threw to Hudson who showed that he can also give change for a dime as he caught the ball near the 15 yard line. He head faked to his right, broke back to his left, and raced into the end zone for an 18 yard touchdown pass play. Mr. W remained perfect, and it was now 44 to 14 with 10:13 left in the third.

At 7:59 left in the third, San Miguel got his revenge. He picked off a Pannell pass and returned it 51 yards for the last Bronco score of the game making it 51 to 14.

Both teams let the reserves get some playing time, and the Dillos scored a touchdown and a safety in the fourth making the final score 51 to 23.

This week the Broncos return to Bronco Stadium to take on the Ozona Lions. Be sure and come to the game to watch the Broncos extract a pound of flesh from the Lions!

Ozona – October 21, 2011

Broncos Tame Lions
By Ray Glasscock

This past Friday night, the Ozona Lions and the Sonora Broncos met for the 87th time. For the second time this season, the Broncos scored more than 50 points against a long time rival and logged the 50th win in the all time series. This was the second time in the series history that Sonora has scored more than 50 points against the Lions. The 1954 Broncos, lead by George Wright and George Johnson, scored 54 points in a game with the Ozona.

One would have expected that this year's Broncos would have been out to gain some revenge on the Lions for the loss to them last year. Yet, it seemed to me that the Broncos expected to score on every series, and they were just playing up to the level that they expect of themselves. The Broncos have won by large margins this year with class.

If the Lions came to Sonora with any hope of winning, it was gone by the end of the fifth play of the game. After the first three plays, the Bronco defense had tackled every Lion runner behind the line of scrimmage, and the Lions punted on fourth and 20.

Clayton Parks brought the Broncos to the line in a wing T type of formation and Edward Garza, as so many Broncos before him, scored on a sweep to the right. Garza's run covered 38 yards.

Kade Wimberley kicked the PAT, and the Broncos had used 10 seconds of clock time for their first scoring drive. 7 to 0 with 9:29 left in the first quarter.

On their next series, the Lions managed to make a first down before being forced to punt. The Lions definitely were not going to let Imoni Cross field and return a punt as they kicked it out of bounds. After Parks was sacked, the Broncos faced a third and long. Cross, the running quarterback, pumped to his right and threw back left to Word Hudson. Hudson had to leap to catch the pass then run to his right across the field for a 55 yard catch and run touchdown.

Mr. W kicked the PAT for the 14 point lead. This possession consisted of three plays and used 1:25 worth of clock time.

Ozona managed a six and out on their next series. The Broncos started on their own 47 yard line. To their credit, the Lion defense stopped the rushing plays on this drive. So, Parks moved the ball by throwing to Zach Badeaux, Cadesman Pope, Dallas Payne, and Cross. Payne, who caught two shovel passes on this drive, got the ball to the one yard line. Coach Sine sent in the heavy package. Parks faked a handoff and threw a one yard touchdown pass to Badeaux. Mr. W boomed the PAT and the Broncos were on their way. Parks completed seven of seven passes on this drive for 53 yards.

Ryan San Miguel made the tackle on the kickoff. Kyle Patlan, who led the Broncos in tackles with 10 (4 solo and 6 assists), smashed the first Lion running play behind the line of scrimmage. On third down, Pope and Badeaux shared a sack forcing another Lion punt.

Sometimes an atta-boy gets followed by an oops. Pope was flagged for roughing the kicker. Three plays later, Damon Evans hit the Lion runner at approximately the same time as the handoff causing a fumble. Jorge Villanueva scooped up the pigskin at the Lion 41 and returned it 30 yards to the Lion 11. Garza smashed his way through the Lions for an eleven yard touchdown run. After a rare miss, the scoreboard read 27 to 0 with 6:00 left in the first half.

The next Lion drive lasted exactly one play. In an attempt to slow down the Bronco pass rush, they tried a screen pass. Under severe pressure by Pope and Evans, the quarterback threw to Sam Powers who raced untouched for a 25 yard pick six.

Mr. W added the PAT upping the score to 34 to 0 with 5:06 left in the half.

Rhett Guerra made the tackle of the kickoff returner. Payne and Patlan combined for a tackle for a loss. On third down, Hudson stepped in front of the receiver and proceeded untouched for another pick six that covered 31 yards. After the PAT, the lead stood at 41 to 0.

The Lions had a change of tactics. Even though they knew that running against the Broncos was impossible, at least they could run four plays before giving the ball back to the Broncos.

The only time that the Broncos failed to score in the first half occurred with a missed 27 yard field goal. However, the drive had covered 69 yards with long receptions and runs by Badeaux plus at leaping catch by Pope. The score at the half was 41 to 0.

On the first drive of the second half, Cross entered at quarterback. Two handoffs to Garza moved the ball from the Bronco 27 yard line to the Lion 43 yard line. Cross ran for ten, followed by a pass to Davis Jimenez who gained 13 yards. Garza took the handoff and ran wide left gaining 19 yards to the Lions six yard line.

Then, one of the strangest series that I have seen lately, started. On first down, a high snap caused Cross to retreat to retrieve the football. As he started to run, he slipped and fell at the 30 yard line. The Broncos were flagged for holding on the next play making it first and goal from the 40 yard line. Erik Santana caught a pass and gained seven yards to the 33. Cross then threw over the middle to Braxton Snyder for a gain to the 12. On fourth and goal, Cross once again found Snyder open over the middle for the touchdown. Mr. W kicked the PAT and the scoreboard read 48 to 0 with 6:57 left in the third.

The last scoring drive belonged to Garza and Santana. Parks handed off or threw and they did the rest. Santana's biggest gain came on a screen pass. Garza blasted up the middle for 25 yards to the Lion one yard line. Santana got the touchdown on a one yard run. Mr. W finished the scoring making the score 55 to 0.

The Lions only bright spot came when they scored on a four yard pass from quarterback Mendez to receiver Mayfield. The final score was 55 to 6. Somewhere there were smiles on the members of the 1942 Ozona Lions team as they beat the 1942 Broncos by a score of 55 to 0.

This week the Broncos travel to Harper to play the Longhorns. Make the drive and support the Broncos as they continue toward an undefeated regular season.

Lions JV – October 20, 2011

Bronco JV Pounds Ozona 30-6
By Nancy Glasscock

After a tie game last week against the San Saba JV team, the JV Broncos had another week to meld the freshmen and sophomores into a combined team. With a few more sophomores moving to varsity, and all of the juniors already playing on Friday night, freshman Andres Acevedo took over the quarterback position full time.

After moving the ball down the field with passes to Sid Anderson, Brett Castillo, and Bryan Garcia plus runs by Castillo and Acevedo, the Lions stopped Sonora on the two yard line (with defensive play calling by the Lion HFC from under the goalposts).

The Broncos got even within one minute. Ethan Patlan broke through the Lions' o-line and tackled the Lion running back in the endzone for a safety with two minutes left in the first quarter. The Bronco JV got the ball back after a Lion three and out. In five plays after a nice Seth Gunn kickoff return, the Broncos got their first touchdown. Castillo opened the drive up with a run. Alfred Rodriguez had three rushes. Acevedo threw a nice touch pass to Castillo in the endzone.

Anderson took the ball in for the two point play. The score was 10-0 at the end of the first quarter.

The Lions and Broncos traded punts in the first half of the second quarter. Chris Rendon hurried the Lion QB who threw the ball to a lineman (a reaction catch). There was no scoring in the second quarter.

The second half started with Acevedo taking the kickoff. This drive had Castillo and Rodriguez moving the ball down the field. Then for the tricky part, Acevedo handed the ball off to Castillo who threw it back to his QB. Acevedo then launched the ball down the middle of the field to a waiting Anderson setting up a first and goal. Castillo lunged in for the second Bronco touchdown. The two point play was no good.

The Broncos got the ball back again after Sonora's defense blitzed. Patlan and Michael Chavez had caused chaos for the Lions' QB and RB. Acevedo then bobbled a snap and the Lions recovered. The Lions had the ball for less than thirty seconds when Anderson got to the Lion punter who also had trouble with the snap. Patlan recovered the ball deep in Lion territory. The third quarter ended with the score 16-0.

The Broncos ran the reverse with Anderson to the 15 yard line. Castillo then swept around the right side of the line for the third Sonora touchdown. The two point play was short of the endzone. Broncos 22 Lions 0.

The next Bronco touchdown came on a defensive play less than 20 seconds after the third touchdown. The Lions' kickoff returner let the ball go over his head, picked it up close to the goal line and was tackled at the seven. Ozona fumbled when either the snap or the handoff was bobbled. Cross recovered the ball at the one foot line and took it into the endzone. The Broncos followed that up with running the heavy formation, and Cross bulled his way through for the two points. The score was Broncos 30 Lions 0 with 8:38 to go in the game.

The Lions scored midway in the fourth quarter, but the Broncos stopped the two point play at the goal line. The final score was 30-6 in favor of the JV Bronco team.

The JV Broncos play the Harper JV this Thursday in Bronco Stadium.

Harper – October 28, 2011

Bronco Express Rolls On
By Ray Glasscock

Again last week, the Broncos dominated a weaker opponent with class as they defeated Harper by a score of 49 to 14. It is hard (possibly impossible) to find a weakness in this year's Broncos. Except for a rare turnover, the Broncos' starters scored on every opportunity with six Broncos scoring points. The average length of the scoring drives was two minutes and three seconds. The average scoring drive lasted four plays, the longest drive was nine plays, and two drives were of the one play variety.

The Bronco defense was just as impressive as the offense. Harper managed two first downs in the first half with one rushing yard and 32 yards of passing! In the first half, Reagan Randle, Harper's fine quarterback, was held to one yard rushing on nine carries. Harper's leading rusher for the game managed 22 yards on six carries.

On the third play of the game, Clayton Parks completed a 65 yard pass to Word Hudson who was forced out of bounds at the Longhorn seven yard line.

Zach Badeaux started in motion from his flanker position, took the handoff from Parks, and ran to his left. Edward Garza took out the defensive back allowing Badeaux to score. Kade Wimberley kicked the PAT and the Broncos led 7 to 0 with 10:33 left in the first quarter.

As usual, the Bronco defense, led by Kyle Patlan, Damon Evans, and Sam Powers forced a three and out. Imoni Cross fielded the punt and started up the left sideline. He was stripped of the ball, but it bounced right to Jorge Villanueva who continued the return to the Longhorn 17 yard line. Dallas Payne accepted the handoff from Parks running to his right.

When he was hemmed in, he cut back to his left and scored. The kick just barely missed to the right, and the score was 13 to 0 with 8:31 left in quarter one.

The Longhorns managed one first down on a completed pass. The drive ended when Davis Jimenez intercepted at midfield. Cross caught a 12 yard pass on fourth down to keep the drive alive. Cadesman Pope caught a short pass and turned it into a 33 gain to Harper's four yard line. After three plays, the Broncos had been backed up to 12 yard line. Parks lofted a pass to Hudson who made his patented, leaping catch for the touchdown. Parks then rolled to his right and threw to Hudson for the two point PAT. With 3:08 left in the first quarter, the Broncos led 21 to 0.

Harper's next drive lasted four plays and ended when Powers recovered a fumble at Harper's 39 yard line. Garza scored on the first play on a run through the Harper defenders. Harper managed to block the PAT, and the scoreboard read Harper 0 – Visitor 27 with 1:56 on the scoreboard clock.

After another three and out, Cross fielded the punt at the 50 yard line and raced for an apparent touchdown. However, it was called back for a block in the back. This drive ended when Randle intercepted a Parks' pass and returned it 30 yards to the Bronco 40 yard line. Four plays later, Payne intercepted Randle.

Hudson hauled in a 35 yard pass to the Longhorn 29 yard line. Pope's catch and run set up a first and goal. Parks hit Badeaux over the middle for a nine yard touchdown. Wimberley boomed the PAT through the uprights for the 34th point with 8:54 left in the second quarter.

The last Bronco scoring drive of the first half lasted eight plays, covered 59 yards and ended with another touchdown pass from Parks to Badeaux. The PAT snap was high and Payne leaped to catch it. The ball bounced off his hands, and Wimberley caught it. He threw a pass that was tipped by Nathan Villa and finally caught by Jesse Vaquera. At first, the officials threw a flag. After they talked about it, the play was allowed to stand as Villa must have been an eligible receiver. The score at the half was 42 to 0.

Harper received the opening kickoff. Will Dutton hustled down the field and tackled the returner at Harper's eight yard line.

Four plays later, Harper was punting from their own end zone. Erik Santana carried three times on the Broncos' last scoring drive, making the last Bronco touchdown on a 31 yard run. Mr. W ended the scoring with his kick. With the score at 49 to 0, the majority of the starters retired to the sideline.

With a running clock, the Bronco reserves gained some valuable experience. The Harper players and fans enjoyed watching their Longhorns score two touchdowns to finish the game at 49 to 14.

Parks completed 17 out of 24 passes for three touchdowns with one interception. Hudson was the leading receiver with four catches for 112 yards and one touchdown. Badeaux was the scoring leader with three touchdowns. Garza and Santana tied for the rushing lead with 41 yards each. Pope logged six tackles with three for losses. Pope and Patlan each had a sack.

The Broncos are now 9 and 0 with one regular season game left. This week, the Coleman Bluecats come to Sonora to play for the outright district championship as both are undefeated in district play. Be sure and come to Bronco Stadium to watch this special group of seniors play their last home game as they seek to become the eighth Bronco team to finish 10 and 0.

Coleman – October 28, 2011

Broncos Are Undefeated District Champions
By Ray Glasscock

When the Broncos took the field last Friday night, they knew that they had the chance to win the District Championship and join the seven previous Bronco teams that finished as 10 and 0 District Champions. At the pep rally, Coach Sine talked about how hard it is to finish with 10 wins and no losses. "I never played on a 10 and 0 team, and, in 20 years of coaching, I have never coached a 10 and 0 team," Sine commented.

The game with the Coleman Bluecats promised to be more interesting than the previous four blowout victories. Coleman had made a remarkable turn around going from 1 and 9 to 7 and 2 with no district losses. As it turned out, the Bluecats played a good game and it was just what the Broncos needed to prepare for the playoffs.

The Bluecats won the toss and elected to defer until the second half. Zach Badeaux returned the opening kickoff to the 30 yard line. The Broncos came to line of scrimmage and opened the game with their longest drive of the season, as they ran 16 plays to travel 70 yards using up 7:23 worth of clock time.

Here are some of the plays from the drive: Edward Garza started with a five yard run, Word Hudson gained 14 on a pass reception, Imoni Cross moved the chains on the quick pass from Clayton Parks, Cadesman Pope earned 13 yards via a pass reception, Cross completed a pass to Hudson, Garza took a pitch from Cross and followed Kade Wimberley 's lead block for a first down, Pope moved the chains on third and long with a tough catch over the middle, the Bluecats were off sides, Cross ran the mis-direction keeper to the one yard line, and Garza got the touchdown on a one yard from the heavy package that featured Wimberley leading the way and Kyle Patlan pulling from his tackle position. (I figured that the longest drive of the season deserved the longest sentence!) Wimberley kicked his first of five PATs making the score 7 to 0 with 4:31 left in the first quarter.

Wimberley, the best Bronco kicker in the past 12 years, boomed it into the end zone for a touchback. The Bluecats, who run the Veer offense, came out running. Damon Evans and Patlan stopped the inside runs and Braxton Snyder turned the attempt to run wide back to inside – another three and out for the Bronco defense.

On the first play, Parks tossed a shovel pass to Badeaux who gained 51 yards before being dragged down. Unfortunately, most of the play was negated by a Bronco penalty. Parks dropped back and threw deep to Hudson on a single receiver play that gained 45 yards to the Bluecats' 27 yard line. However, the wheels came off as Cross lost yardage on a high snap, and Parks fumbled as he was forced to scramble.

The Bluecats had good field position started from their 43 yard line. Three running plays later, the Bluecats faced a fourth and one at the Bronco 48 yard line. The

Bluecat quarterback JUST made it on the midline keeper. They followed their first first down of the game with two more. Then, their best runner had to leave the game with a hyper-extended knee after one of his lineman rolled onto his knee as Patlan made the tackle. (From the video, it is a wonder that he didn't break his leg.) Coach Ballard called two passing plays that went incomplete, and the Broncos took over on downs.

Badeaux sprinted up the middle for a 24 yard gain.

Garza followed with a run of 16 yards. A double reverse resulted in an eight yard gain by Cross. Parks scrambled to his left to avoid the rushers and threw a strike to Cross at the 15 yard line.

After a five yard penalty, Cross dropped to pass, saw daylight, and sprinted through the Bluecats for a 20 yard touchdown. Mr. W made it 14 to 0 at the half. This scoring drive covered 70 yards in seven plays and lasted 2:24.

The third quarter started with the Broncos kicking to the Bluecats, but the quarter belonged to the Broncos. Without their best runner, the ineffective Bluecat rushing game got even worse. After three plays of going backwards, the Coleman punter had to kick into the strong south wind. The punt landed near the Bluecat 45 yard line and bounced perfectly into the sure hands of Cross. He turned on the burners and sped down the right sideline for a touchdown. Another booming PAT by Mr. W and the Broncos had upped their lead to 21 points with 9:31 left in the third quarter.

Mr. W logged another touchback to his list of kicking accomplishments. After two running plays lost yardage, Coleman completed their first and only pass of the game for a one yard loss.

The Broncos started their next drive in Coleman territory at their 43 yard line. After Pope picked up the first down on a catch and run from Parks, the Coleman defense forced the Broncos into a fourth and long.

Hudson ran the button hook and Parks hit him for the first down. Parks started the option play by running off tackle and pitched it to Badeaux. He made a one handed catch and sprinted into the end zone for a 15 yard rushing touchdown. After the PAT, the score stood at 28 to 0 with 5:01 left in the third.

Once again the incredible Bronco defense forced another 3 and out. After two incomplete passes, Parks dropped back and tossed a screen pass to Garza for an 18 yard gain. The next pass was to Badeaux who gained 15 yards. Parks threw to Hudson who broke tackles with his patented spin move for an 18 yard touchdown. After the PAT, the scoreboard read 35 to 0.

While the scoring was over, the fourth quarter featured several long runs by Garza and some more Bronco defense. To the Bluecats' credit, they managed to put on a multi-play drive to the Bronco ten yard. Powers recovered a fumble and ended their best drive of the night. When the clock struck 0:00, the 2011 Broncos joined the 10 and 0 club founded by the 1956, 1961, 1965, 1966, 1971, 1999, and 2000 Sonora Broncos!

As District Champions, the Broncos will have a bye. Their Area opponent will be the winner of the bi-district game between the Weimar Wildcats and Rivera Kaufer

Seahawks who play in Victoria Memorial Stadium on Saturday, November 12th at 2 PM. Weimar is 6 and 4 and Rivera Kaufer is 9 and 1. Weimar is Coach Sine's hometown and Rivera Kaufer is one of Refugio's blowout victims as they lost to the Bobcats by a score of 81 to 6.

Area Champions – Weimar – November 11, 2011

Sonora Broncos – 11-0 Area Champions
Sonora 31 – Weimar 0
By Ray Glasscock

For the first time since 2003, the Sonora Broncos are the Class 2A Division II Area Champions as they defeated the Weimar Wildcats 31 to 0 last Friday in Marble Falls. The Broncos entered the game as undefeated District Champions after a two week layoff due to a first round Bye.

For the first time this season, not everything went the Broncos way on the offensive side of ball. The Broncos lost two fumbles and had two interceptions. They had five trips into the red zone that ended with zero points: twice on downs, one missed field goal, one lost fumble and the half ended as the Broncos tried to line up for a field goat attempt.

However, as in all previous games, the Bronco defense came to play and totally dominated the Weimar's offense. Sonora held the Wildcats to only one first down in the first half and four first downs in the second half. The Wildcats completed 4 of 16 passes for 30 yards, and they ran the ball 32 times for 54 yards! Weimar's BJ Jones, who had rushed for over 1,000 yards this season, managed 50 yards on 21 carries. The Broncos had 18 solo tackles with the rest being the "herd of Broncos" type of tackles. Imoni Cross and Dallas Payne had three solos each. Hagen Kennedy, Braxton Snyder, Sam Powers, and Cadesman Pope had two solos. Snyder and Powers had quarterback sacks. Jorge Villanueva and Damon Evans each recovered Wildcat fumbles and Payne recovered TWO of their fumbles.

The Broncos won the toss and elected to receive. The Broncos' first play was the pitch sweep to Edward Garza. Against Ozona, this play went for a touchdown. Against a playoff team, it went for two yards. Clayton Parks used the quick pass to Zach Badeaux on the flanker screen. Badeaux gained 24 yards after the catch. Two plays later, the exchange between Cross and Badeaux resulted in a fumble that Weimar recovered.

Weimar attempted a first play pass. Pope blitzed and hit their quarterback just as he was throwing causing an incomplete pass. Three plays later, Cross fielded their punt at the 10 yard line and returned it 26 yards. The Wildcat defense stepped up and forced a three and out for Sonora.

Sonora returned the favor, and this time Cross returned their punt 21 yards to the Wildcats' 48 yard line. Parks rolled to his left and threw deep for Pope. Pope made a leaping catch at the Wildcats' 16 yard line for a 32 yard completion.

Garza slipped through their defensive line for a ten yard gain. Three plays later, Kade Wimberley kicked a 25 yard field goal to give the Broncos all the points that they would need for the victory. The 3 to 0 score came with 3:17 left in the first quarter.

Davis Jimenez and Pope hustled down and tackled the kickoff returner at their 20 yard line. Once again, the Bronco defense held and forced another punt. The next Bronco drive featured another great catch by Pope, but it ended with a turnover on downs.

Payne ended the Wildcat drive on its first play as he recovered a Weimar fumble at Weimar's thirty yard line.

Parks to a leaping Pope moved the chains to the 16 yard line. Badeaux hauled in a pass and was pushed out of bounds at the seven yard line. This promising trip into the red zone ended at the seven yard after an incomplete fourth down pass.

After the next Wildcat punt, the Broncos started at their 40 yard line. After hitting Word Hudson on a third down pass for a first down, Parks rolled to his left. Hudson signaled to Parks that he was open and Parks threw a perfect pass to Hudson in the end zone for the first Bronco touchdown.

The scoring play covered 32 yards. After Wimberley kicked the PAT, the Broncos had a ten point lead with 5:01 left in the second quarter.

Weimar managed to make a first down before fumbling to the Broncos.

With time running out, Parks and Hudson connected three times to move the ball into the red zone.

Parks threw to Cross who appeared to have made a diving catch in the end zone. A frame by frame replay of my video showed that the ball hit the ground, and the official's call of incomplete pass was correct. After a complete pass to Badeaux with no timeouts left, the field goal team hurried onto the field but could not get the kick off before the half ended. The score at the end of the half was Sonora 10 and Weimar 0.

Sonora kicked off but the Bronco defense forced Weimar into a turnover on downs at their 35 yard line giving the Broncos a short field. The Weimar defense stepped up and stopped the Bronco running plays forcing Sonora into a fourth down try for a first down. Parks completed a pass over the middle to Hudson for 13 yards and a first down.

However this drive stalled due to penalties. Wimberley attempted a field goal that was short. BJ Jones returned the ball 30 yards to their 30 yard line.

On Weimar's third play, they attempted the option play to their left. Snyder broke through the line and hit the quarterback as he was pitching the ball. When Jones dropped the ball, Payne fell on the ball for the Broncos.

This opportunity to score ended when Garza broke a big gain up the middle, but a hard hit caused a fumble through the back of the end zone resulting in a touchback for the Wildcats.

The Wildcats returned the favor two plays later when Jones fumbled again and Evans recovered for the Broncos. This drive ended when Parks tried an underhanded pass to Pope that was intercepted by the Wildcats.

Kyle Patlan and Jorge Villanueva broke through the huge Wildcat offensive line for a tackle for a loss.

After the next Wildcat punt, with one second left, Parks threw long to Hudson over the middle who caught the ball near the five yard line and, once again, walked into the end zone. Wimberley's kick was good and the score was 17 to 0 at the end of the third quarter.

In the fourth quarter, the Bronco running game started working. Zach Badeaux scored on a 35 yard run on a flanker mis-direction play. After the PAT, the score was 24 to 0 with 5:27 left in the game.

On the last Bronco drive, Garza carried the ball play after play. He got the last touchdown on a five yard run. Mr. W kicked the PAT and the final score of the game occurred with 1:15 left in the game.

Hudson led all receivers for the game with 10 receptions and 154 yards. Garza was the leading rusher with 78 yards on 17 carries.

Parks completed 18 of 35 passes for 283 yards for 2 touchdowns and 2 interceptions. For the season, Parks has completed 162 of 246 passes for 2529 yards and 26 touchdowns. Parks how holds the Bronco single season passing yardage record as he passed the 2459 yards amassed by Bryce Williams during the 2000 season. He needs five more touchdown passes to tie Williams' 2000 season total of 31 touchdowns.

This week the Broncos play a rematch with the East Bernard Brahmas at 12:00 noon Saturday in the Alamodome. Get your popcorn ready and come to see the Broncos play their very first playoff game in an indoor stadium.

East Bernard - November 26, 2011

Sonora Broncos – Region IV Semi-Final Champions
Sonora 28 – East Bernard 27

By Ray Glasscock

Ice water must be flowing through the Broncos veins! Many teams lose their focus when they get to stay in a fancy hotel on the San Antonio Riverwalk, get to watch a couple of 4A /5A playoff games in the Alamodome, and then walk onto the field to play the first Bronco game ever in the Alamodome. While the highs and lows of this game caused elation and fear among the fans, the Broncos never lost their focus with the swings of football fortune.

The East Bernard Brahmas won the toss and deferred to the second half. Imoni Cross returned the opening kickoff to midfield. The first Bronco drive of the game lasted 3:04 minutes and covered 51 yards. On the sixth play of the drive, a Bronco penalty forced a third and 18. Cross rolled to his right and then threw a throw back screen to Zach Badeaux.

Badeaux ran through tacklers for the first down. On the eighth play of the drive, Clayton Parks found Word Hudson splitting the Brahmas' defense for a 24 yard touchdown pass. Kade Wimberley kicked the PAT for the early 7 to 0 lead with 8:48 left in the first quarter.

Wimberley boomed the kickoff into the end zone for a touchback. The Sonora fans were holding their breaths wondering if Ty Slanina, the Brahma quarterback, could be contained. The Brahma opening drive lasted 8 plays. Slanina gained seven yards on the second play, 15 yards on the third play, 31 yards on the fourth play. Facing third and short at the Bronco 32 yard line, Slanina rolled to his right looking for a receiver and Cross forced him out of bounds after a two yard gain. On fourth and short, he ran to his left and Dallas Payne tackled him short of the first down. Bronco fans felt a little better.

East Bernard forced a three and out and Parks punted. Justin McGuire reeled off the best punt return against the Broncos this year as he ran 25 yards to the Bronco 29 yard line. Three plays later, Slanina rolled to his right and Cross and Hudson ran him out of bounds at the Broncos' 13 yard line. A five yard penalty set up a 1st and 15. Sam Powers and Chance Campbell tacked Jontrey Goff for no gain. Joc Richardson tried the middle where Powers, Payne, and Campbell stopped him for a one yard gain.

On second down, Campbell and Cross smashed Slanina for no gain. On third down, Kyle Patlan broke through the Brahma line and forced Slanina to scramble. Campbell was about to make a tackle for a loss when Slanina threw the ball away. Quinton Farris attempted a 27 yard field goal that missed by inches at 1:08 left in the first quarter.

During Sonora's next drive, Parks threw deep to Cross. It was ruled an interception even though Cross and the East Bernard player had simultaneous possession of the ball. The tension in the Bronco stands was beginning to build.

Slanina handed the ball to Goff who ran off tackle to his left. After four yards, Braxton Snyder reached in and stripped the ball, and Payne recovered for the Broncos on our 45 yard line. On the first play of the second quarter, Cross took the snap as quarterback, threw a lateral to Parks, and Parks completed a pass to Cross for a ten yard gain. Parks completed another screen pass; this time to Edward Garza who hit and bounced, bounced and hit for an eight yard gain setting up a third and short at the Brahmas' 27 yard line. With everyone expecting the heavy package, Parks brought the Broncos to the line in the spread formation. Parks handed the ball to Badeaux. Patlan dropped back and pancaked the defensive end allowing Badeaux an eleven yard gain and a first down at the 16 yard line.

Badeaux got the second Bronco touchdown on his third consecutive carry. The touchdown run covered five yards through the middle of their line. Wimberley kicked the PAT, and the Broncos led 14 to 0 with 10:31 left in the second quarter.

McGuire returned the kickoff to the 25 yard line where Erik Santana and Campbell made the tackle. They ripped off two nice runs until Powers blitzed and sacked Slanina for a loss. Slanina handed to Goff who was tackled by Patlan and Campbell for no gain. Slanina dropped to pass. Cadesman Pope forced him to reverse field and Campbell sacked him for a nine yard loss. The Brahma punter got off a bad punt that gave the Broncos good field position at our 38 yard line. Badeaux started in motion from his flanker position and took the pitch from Parks gaining eleven yards and a first down at our 49 yard line.

Over 1900 people on YouTube have already watched the next play. Parks threw a quick flanker screen pass to Cross. Cross amazed everyone at the game and thousands on the internet as he broke over eight tackles enroute to a fifty yard gain - one yard shy of the end zone. Coach Sine sent in the heavy package. Parks handed the ball to Badeaux. Michael Sanchez and Lino Villanueva double teamed the nose guard. Pope blocked left on the tackle, and Damon Evans blocked the cornerback. Badeaux used his speed to make it into the end zone before the linebacker arrived. Wimberley kicked the PAT, and the Broncos led 21 to 0 with 6:06 left in the second quarter. The Bronco crowd felt a little better as things were really going the Broncos' way.

Evans, Campbell, and Payne made consecutive solo tackles, and East Bernard had to punt. The Broncos moved the chains after a leaping catch by Pope. Two plays later, big mo changed and how. Parks dropped to pass. A rushing Brahma pushed Cross backwards knocking the ball out of Parks' hand. The Brahmas recovered. Six plays later, they had a first and ten in the Broncos' red zone. The Broncos held for three plays, but, on fourth and one, Slanina ran to his right and made it into the end zone for East Bernard's first touchdown. Farris kicked the PAT and the score at the half was 21 to 7 in favor of Sonora.

Sonora kicked off to start the second half. The Brahmas used six plays to move 75 yards for their second touchdown. With the Broncos stacking the line to stop Slanina, he dropped back and threw a 37 yard touchdown pass to McGuire. After the PAT, the Brahmas trailed by only a touchdown and definitely had the momentum. There was 9:12 left in the third quarter.

After one first down earned by a scrambling Cross, the Broncos were forced to punt. The fired up Brahma offensive line began to open holes as the Broncos allowed three consecutive first down runs. On the fourth play of the drive, Slanina broke into the open and appeared on his way to score when Campbell caught him and tackled him. Two plays later, Richardson scored on a three yard run. McGuire's PAT tied the score at 21 each 4:18 left in the third quarter.

Badeaux returned the kickoff to the 22 yard line. With the East Bernard crowd going absolutely crazy, Parks trotted onto the field to start the drive of the season. He threw to Pope, and then to Cross. He had to scramble and ducked under a sure tackle to hit Hudson over the middle. A quick toss to Badeaux resulted in ten yards and a first down. The next play was an incomplete pass. A quick pass to Payne gained more yardage after a great block by Hudson – another first down. Parks threw to Cross for a short gain. Parks was forced to scramble and he gained about five yards. East Bernard tackled Parks on a coverage sack. On fourth and three, Parks took the snap and began looking for a receiver. With his primary receiver covered, he spotted Davis Jimenez open and fired him the ball. Just as Riley Crain did in the 2000 State Championship game, Jimenez went to his knees to catch the ball and keep the drive alive. Frame by frame of my high definition video showed that Davis was on his knees and leaned forwarded to catch the ball. He got his hands under the ball and, if there had been an NFL replay, the call on the field would have stood. With the pocket collapsing, Parks ran straight ahead, and just before crossing the line of scrimmage, fired a strike to Badeaux at the three yard line.

Two plays later, Badeaux took the pitch and ran wide to his right for what turned out to be the game winning touchdown.

Wimberley kicked the PAT, and the Broncos led 28 to 21 with 25 seconds left in the third quarter. Parks completed eight of nine passes on the 77 yard drive that lasted 3:47. All Bronco fans let out a sigh of relief, but we all knew there was still a quarter to play.

In fact, it only took East Bernard four plays and 1:07 to score their last touchdown. With the Broncos stacking the line to stop Slanina, he faked a run and threw a 58 yard touchdown pass to Goff. Farris came onto the field to tie the game. However, he kicked it low, bouncing it off one of his own linemen. The score was 28 to 27 in favor of the Broncos.

The next drive of the Broncos featured Parks to Pope.

Three big catch and runs by Pope gave the Broncos a first and goal at the Brahmas' five yard line. On third down, Cross rolled to his right and spotted Hudson open in the end zone. Number 65 of the Brahmas jumped and just managed to tip the pass causing it to fall incomplete. Parks threw incomplete on fourth down and East Bernard took over on their own five yard line.

Slanina left the game temporarily after tweaking his ankle. East Bernard picked up three first downs to get away from their end zone. With time running out, they had to abandon their running game. On fourth down, a low snap to Slanina caused him to scramble and Evans chased him out of bounds short of the first down. With 2:12 left, it looked like the game was finally out of the Brahmas' reach.

But East Bernard still had all three of their time outs. On the third play of the Broncos' drive to run out the clock, Cross handed off to Garza who raced around the left end and into the end zone. However, the touchdown was called back on a holding penalty. Two plays later, Badeaux and Parks didn't get a clean exchange and the Brahmas recovered at their 27 yard line.

East Bernard needed to go 73 yards with one timeout left. Slanina's first pass was incomplete. Then Payne delivered another "slobberknocker" hit causing the receiver to drop the ball. On third down, Slanina's pass was too high and uncatchable. East Bernard called their last time to discuss their fourth down play. Hudson ended the Brahmas' last chance when he batted their last pass away from the receiver and into the middle of the field.

Parks completed 23 of 29 passes for 256 yards on one touchdown. Badeaux led all rushers with 56 yards on ten carries. Cross caught six passes for 82 yards, Hudson had five receptions for 37 yards, and Pope had 78 yards on five catches. Jimenez had one season saving catch for 12 yards.

On defense, Campbell led all tacklers with 4 solo and 12 assisted tackles. Payne, Cross, Hudson, Powers, and Patlan had double digit tackles. Powers and Campbell each had a sack.

This week the 12 and 0 Broncos play the 12 and 0 Refugio Bobcats for the Region IV Championship. The game will be played at Heroes Stadium in San Antonio on Friday night at 7:30.

Refugio – December 9, 2011

Sonora Broncos Finish Best Season in Ten Years
By Ray Glasscock

This past Friday night at Heroes Stadium in San Antonio, the Refugio Bobcats were awarded the trophy for the Class 2A – Division II – Region IV Championship based on the number of points on the final scoreboard. While they outscored the Broncos by a score of 41 to 24, they left the field with some "firsts" of their own. For the first time all season, they left the field in the first half with only three first downs and 63 yards of offense. For the game, they had fewer first downs than the other team, plus never before had any team kept all three of their outstanding rushers below a hundred yards. The Broncos also held them to only 82 yards of passing offense.

In the first half, the Bobcats scored on the second play of the game and the next to the last play of the first half. Both were basically defensive touchdowns. Sonora scored a touchdown in the second quarter on an eight play 40 yard drive. Clayton Parks completed passes to Zach Badeaux and Imoni Cross.

Cross had a 15 yard catch and run that also drew a late hit out of bounds penalty giving the Broncos a first and goal from the five. Cross got the touchdown on a sweep to the left. A high snap prevented a successful PAT.

The game slipped away from the Broncos in the last half of the third quarter and the first three minutes of the fourth quarter. During that time, the Bobcats scored on a screen pass and three rushing touchdowns to take a 41 to 6 lead with 5:10 left in the game. I am sure that the Refugio crowd expected that the Broncos would fold and their Bobcats would once again win by 40 or more points.

After they kicked off to the Broncos, their offensive team never touched the ball again. The Broncos scored their second touchdown of the game on a nine play 88 yard drive. Cross got the touchdown on a 41 yard run. The two point PAT failed.

Cross executed a perfect onsides kick that Davis Jimenez recovered. With 2:36 left in the game, Parks led the Broncos on a seven play 45 yard drive that ended with a two yard touchdown pass to Word Hudson. Pope was the victim for a bad call as the referee clearly missed a pass interference on the PAT attempt.

With 26 seconds left in the game, Cross once again executed a perfect onsides kick that Hudson caught in full stride and he almost took it all the way. With two seconds left the game, Parks threw to Hudson who lateralled to Cross. Cross finished the 30 yard scoring play as he raced untouched into the end zone as the time expired on the best Bronco season in ten years.

Parks completed 20 for 42 passes for 230 yards and two touchdowns. Cross was the leading rusher with 62 yards on 13 carries with two runs going for touchdowns.

Hudson caught five passes for 67 yards and one touchdown. Cross caught four passes for 52 yards and one touchdown (sharing with Hudson on the lateral I suppose.) Badeaux had four catches for 38 yards, Edward Garza snagged three for 25 yards, Dallas Payne caught one for nine yards, and Cadesman Pope had four for 49 yards.

Payne led all tacklers with four solo and 14 assists. Damon Evans had 12 tackles and Sam Powers had 10. Kyle Patlan had a quarterback sack.

Imoni Cross finished his high school career with the game of his life. Cross had three passes defended, two interceptions, seven tackles, and three of the four touchdowns.

Next week, I will summarize this outstanding season to ensure the history of the 2011 Sonora Broncos will be documented for future generations.

2011 Football Season Recap

2011 Sonora Broncos Make History
By Ray Glasscock

I want to make sure the people of Sonora truly appreciate the accomplishments of the 2011 Sonora Broncos. The cliché that best and most accurately describes this year's Broncos is this: "The team's accomplishments was greater than the sum of the players' individual accomplishments."

The Broncos finished with a 12 and 1 record. The only teams that won twelve games in a row are the 1966, 1971, 1999, and 2000 teams. The 1968, 1969, 1970, and 2001 teams all won twelve or more with some losses breaking the consecutive string.

The 2011 Broncos scored 538 points for a 41.4 point per game average which is the highest all time. The 2000 Broncos averaged 39.5 for second place. The 455 points that the Broncos scored in the regular season is the all time regular season scoring record. They passed for 250.7 yards per game, rushed for 134.7 yards per game, made 101.5 tackles, and sacked the opposing quarterback 1.9 times per game.

Several Broncos did set some all time Bronco records.

Clayton Parks set the all time season passing yardage record with 3015 yards. He threw for 29 touchdowns which is two short of Bryce Williams' record of 31 in the 2000 season.

Word Hudson is Sonora's all time leading receiver with 2215 yards on 141 receptions. Noe Chavez is the all time single season receiver with 1233 yards on 58 catches. Noe played on the 1966 State Champions.

Kade Wimberley kicked four field goals which is the most field goals in the past ten years and is possibly an all time record. He finished with 67 kicking points which is one point short of Javier Gaytan's all time record of 68.

Edward Garza was the rushing leader this year with 705 yards on 102 carries for a 6.91 yard per carry average.

Imoni Cross, Zach Badeaux, Cadesman Pope caught 30, 40, and 40 passes respectively.

Dallas Payne led all tacklers with 139 followed by Damon Evans with 130, and Cross with 119.

Sam Powers was the sack leader with six.

Cross was the interception leader with six picks.

Badeaux led all scorers with 114 points and 19 touchdowns.

All of Sonora thanks Coach Sine and his coaching staff for leading our Broncos to an amazing season!

Post Season Honors

2011 All West Texas

SAN ANGELO, Texas — For two years, Clayton Parks patiently waited on the sidelines for his turn to step onto the football field as the starting quarterback for Sonora High School.

Once he finally got his chance, the senior signal-caller turned in a record-setting performance, leading the Broncos to an undefeated regular season and four rounds deep into the playoffs.

Sonora's run ended with its only loss to eventual undefeated champion Refugio in the state quarterfinals, but with his breakout season, Parks solidified himself as the

Standard-Times All-West Texas Class 2A MVP.

"It was what I had always dreamed of," Parks said. "I knew this season was going to be my only shot. I just put it in my mind to take the opportunity and make the most of it. I just wanted to go out there and show what I had."

Parks accomplished his mission, completing 205 of his 317 pass attempts for 3,015 yards and 29 touchdowns in his only season as the starter.

Coming up through the program, he had looked up to former Bronco quarterback Bryce Williams, who led Sonora to a state title in 2000. His sophomore and junior seasons were spent watching as last year's 2A co-MVP Ethan Morriss brought Sonora back to relevancy.

Parks took it one step further.

When it was finally his turn to take the snaps, he shattered Williams' 11-year-old single-season passing record by more than 500 yards and guided the Broncos on their deepest postseason run since that 2000 championship season.

Sonora head coach David T. Sine knew what Parks was capable of heading into the season, and he adjusted his offense accordingly.

"At a small school, you have to adjust your offense based on the talent that you have. You have to be willing to change," said Sine, who earned Co-Coach of the Year honors leading the Broncos to a 12-1 record. "With Clayton, he's a student of the game. He understands the game, and his intelligence level allows us to send five guys out in the route.

"All five guys are running their route full speed because they don't know who's going to get the ball, and our offensive line did a great job of protecting him."

Parks' 3,015 passing yards were spread out among a number of receivers this season, led by senior Word Hudson, who hauled in 16 of his quarterback's 29 touchdown passes.

Hudson surpassed the 1,000-yard mark in receiving each of the past two seasons, and with Parks throwing the ball this year he became the Broncos' all-time leading receiver.

"Clayton was under a lot of pressure playing behind one of the best players to ever come through Sonora," Hudson said. "But he was real accurate, and real calm and collected. He could throw a bad pass or get hit real hard and bounce right back.

"We called him our Drew Brees. He was just like Brees the way he handled the game. Clayton knew the defenses and just had a knack for throwing the ball. He knew just where to put it."

His accuracy was among the best in the state, completing 65 percent of his throws (205 of 317), and Parks was intercepted only 10 times — or once for every 32 times he aired it out.

But he humbly shook off the credit, praising Hudson, Imoni Cross, Cadesman Pope and Zach Badeaux among the other talented players surrounding him.

"It's amazing getting to play with those kind of athletes," Parks said. "It was unbelievable the talent I had around me to help me reach my goals.

"I didn't think I was going to put up those kind of numbers, but I felt like I could come close to the record. With those guys, I knew I had a shot at it if I could just get the ball in their hands."

Sine said he has coached some "great" quarterbacks in his 20-year career — including Morriss and 1998 Heisman runner-up Michael Bishop of Kansas State.

"Clayton is different," he said. "Just with the amount of time he spent and his work ethic in the weight room. On the mental side of the game, he's the best that I've ever coached.

"Clayton was on a mission, and it's really nice to see a young man set goals and accomplish those goals."

MVP

Clayton Parks, Sonora

Senior, 5-9, 170

Parks was named the District 13-2A Offensive MVP after leading Sonora to an undefeated regular season and four rounds deep into the playoffs. The senior signal-caller threw for a school-record 3,015 yards and 29 touchdowns in his first year as the starter, while completing more than 65 percent of his passes.

Co-Coaches of the Year

David Sine, Sonora

In just his third season in Sonora, Sine guided the Broncos to a perfect 10-0 regular season, captured the 13-2A title, and was named the district's Coach of the Year. The Broncos made it to the state quarterfinals before falling to eventual state champion Refugio, ending the year with a 12-1 record.

Houston Guy, Wall

Guy's Flexbone offense produced some of the biggest numbers in recent history for the Wall Hawks, who won the District 2-2A crown, and reached to regional round of the playoffs, before losing 15-14 to Eastland. Guy earned 2-2A Coach of the Year honors after guiding the Hawks to an 11-1 record.

Wide Receivers

Word Hudson, Sonora

Senior, 6-0, 170

Hudson was a threat to score each time he caught the ball in his senior season. The two-way all-district selection totaled 1,007 yards on 59 receptions and scored 16 touchdowns. He became Sonora's all-time leading receiver with 2,208 yards in his career.

Tight End

Cadesman Pope, Sonora

Senior, 6-5, 185

The 6-foot-5 tight end towered over most defensive backs as part of Sonora's aerial assault. Despite also being heavily relied on for his blocking skills, Pope still caught 40 passes for 755 yards — over 18 yards per reception — and scored four touchdowns.

Offensive Linemen

Kyle Patlan, Sonora

Senior, 5-10, 220

Patlan was the leader of an offensive line that paved the way for the Broncos' 5,010 yards of offense. He graded out at better than 85 percent for the season with 12 pancake blocks and did not allow a single sack.

Defensive Linemen

Damon Evans, Sonora

Junior, 5-11, 190

Evans made his presence felt with 130 tackles, three sacks and three forced fumbles from his spot on the Sonora defensive line. He also was credited with seven quarterback hurries and three fumble recoveries.

Linebackers

Jorge Villanueva, Sonora

Senior, 5-9, 175

Villanueva recorded 107 tackles at linebacker for the Broncos this season and was selected 1st team, all-district. He forced four fumbles and recovered two others while playing a major role in Sonora's defense.

Defensive backs

Imoni Cross, Sonora

Senior, 5-10, 170

Cross was an all-state choice after making 119 tackles with six interceptions, one returned for a touchdown. He was a dangerous return man, with four touchdowns (two kickoff returns and two punt returns) and played a large role in the Broncos' offense.

Dallas Payne, Sonora

Senior, 5-11, 165

Another all-state selection for Sonora, Payne tallied 139 tackles this season, with one sack and two interceptions, returning one of them for a score. The senior defensive back also forced four fumbles and recovered four.

Kicker

Kade Wimberley, Sonora

Junior, 6-1, 225

Wimberley's powerful leg totaled 4,367 yards on kickoffs — 51.4 per kick — with seven touchbacks. He made 55 extra points and four field goals this season, with a long of 38 yards. Wimberley was named 13-2A Special Teams MVP.

Utility Back

Zach Badeaux, Sonora

Senior, 5-11, 175

Badeaux was the definition of a utility for the Broncos in this season. The senior rushed 56 times for 350 yards and 13 touchdowns, and caught 40 passes for 532 yards and six more scores. Defensively he recorded 90 tackles, three sacks and one interception.

2011 Statistics

Passing

Player	Comp	Att	Yards	C%	Y/G	TD	Int	Rate
Parks	205	317	3015	64.7%	231.9	29	10	113
Cross	11	17	205	64.7%	15.8	3	1	121
Jimenez	3	9	31	33.3%	2.4	0	0	44
Team	221	348	3259	63.0%	250.7	32	11	112

Rushing

Player	Carries	Yards	Average	Y/G	TDs
E. Garza	102	705	6.91	54.2	9
I. Cross	68	425	6.25	32.7	6
Z. Badeaux	56	350	6.25	26.9	13
S. Gonzales	9	47	5.22	15.7	0
J. Vasquez	13	46	3.54	5.8	0
D. Payne	3	25	8.33	1.9	1
K. Wimberley	4	18	4.5	1.4	2
W. Hudson	1	8	8	.6	0
W. Dutton	6	8	1.33	1,6	0
C. Parks	43	-103	-2.4	-7.9	1
Team	348	1751	5.03	134.7	36

Receiving

Player	Rec	Yards	Average	Y/G	TDs
W. Hudson	59	1007	17.07	77.5	16
C. Pope	40	755	18.88	58.1	4
Z. Badeaux	40	532	13.30	40.9	6
I. Cross	30	383	12.77	29.5	3
E. Garza	21	203	9.67	15.6	1
D. Payne	10	116	11.60	8.9	1
D. Jimenez	7	114	16.29	8.8	0
B. Snyder	4	57	14.25	4.8	1
E. Santana	3	48	15.33	3.8	0
R. San Miguel	3	22	7.33	1.8	0

R. Guerra	3	17	5.67	2.8	0
W. Dutton	1	7	7.00	1.4	0
Team	221	3259	14.75	250.7	65

Tackles

Player	Solo	Asst	Tot Tckls	T/G	TFL
D. Payne	21	118	139	10.7	2.0
D. Evans	22	108	130	10.0	7.0
I. Cross	17	102	119	9.2	2.0
J. Villanueva	13	94	107	8.2	6.0
S. Powers	9	90	99	7.6	5.0
K. Patlan	15	78	93	7.2	10.0
Z. Badeaux	14	76	90	6.9	5.0
C. Pope	19	51	70	5.4	10.0
R. San Miguel	12	55	67	5.6	1.0
W. Hudson	19	47	66	5.1	2.0
E. Santana	11	48	59	4.9	5.0
C. Campbell	5	30	35	7.0	3.0
R. Snyder	18	25	34	2.8	2.0
Team	228	1092	1320	101.5	62.0

Scoring

Player	TDs	Conversions	Kick Pts	Total
Z. Badeaux	19	0	0	114
W. Hudson	17			102
K.Wimberley	2	2	67	81
I. Cross	12		1	73
E. Garza	10	4		66
C. Pope	4	2		26
D. Payne	3			18

E. Santana	3			18
R. San Miguel	1			6
S. Powers	1			6
Team	76	12	68	538

Kade Wimberley kicked 55 extra points out of 65 tries. He made four of 8 field goals for a total of 67 points.

This group of athletes also had a 27 and 9 record in baseball and advanced to the Region I finals.

They won district and regional in track and finished in fourth place at the state track meet.

Lightning Source UK Ltd.
Milton Keynes UK
UKRC011922180119
335576UK00004BA/38